Even The Crazy Man Wept
Reflections following the War in Cambodia

Dr Edwin Pugh

Dr Edwin Pugh

First edition (CreateSpace Edition 2015)

e-mail: enquiries@movements.me.uk
websites: www.movements.me.uk
www.transformhealthcarecambodia.org.uk

Published by Sharp Edge Publishing - *'Movements'* 2015
UK Edition © Sharp Edge Publishing - *'Movements'* 2015
Text © Dr Edwin Pugh 2015
Cover photograph © Dr Edwin Pugh

Contents

Beginnings

Recommendation

I strongly recommend this deeply thought provoking book with its powerful and poignant collection of true stories from 'the life of Bob', a Jesuit brother who literally, 'walked the walk' and 'talked the talk' with victims of the war in Cambodia. It is also an intensely personal reflection of this man who has committed his life to stay with these survivors of the notorious Cambodian genocide during their return to their war-ravaged and mine-infested homeland and to serve them as they languished in the so-called safety of refugee camps.

He is among them still. Through his eyes the reader is compelled to see the evils of that war, the pain and indignity suffered by those compelled to exist as refugees and the urgent need for peace and reconciliation.

Baroness Caroline Cox

Baroness Caroline Cox has been Deputy Speaker of the House of Lords, and is founder of the humanitarian agency HART (Humanitarian Aid Relief Trust). She is respected as a tireless campaigner for social justice and for helping in troubled and 'forgotten' parts of the world.

About the Book

This book challenges the reader to see, in response to the genocide in Cambodia and its aftermath, compassion, sadness, love and righteous anger expressed by a remarkable man who shared his life with the poor during this time. The events and names in this book are real.

For over 30 years Bob, a Jesuit Brother, has committed his life to living among the poor of Cambodia. He has been with them during their plight as refugees in camps on the Thai - Cambodian border. He has lived and 'walked' with them on the fearful return into their war-ravaged homeland. He has seen and experienced 'first-hand' the effect the war - and 'peace'- has had on them. He is with them now.

Bob wrote down these experiences. He wrote down his inner soul-searching response to the inhumanity of war and its consequences to individual lives.

This book is a compilation of Bob's writings. They are unique. They are personal. They are deeply challenging. Many are an uncensored cry from the heart; anguish from a spiritual man seeking to challenge the evil of war and bring love and peace to mankind.

Finally, in respect to Bob it needs to be stated that this book is not about him! That would be the last thing he would want or agree to. Instead the book is about situations in the world that should not be tolerated. It is hoped these personal tales and reflections can inspire the reader, whoever you may be, to be a peacemaker.

We cannot be 'Bob' but we can learn from his selfless service of love to others.

It's a remarkable lesson - a lesson for today.

About the Book's Editor

Dr. Edwin Pugh has a longstanding involvement in Cambodia.

He and his wife, Kim, lived and worked on the Thai-Cambodian border for two years (1990-1991).

As part of a United Nations relief effort they helped provide health services to Khmer refugees. Since then Edwin has done many further consultancy visits to Cambodia.

From 2008 Edwin and Kim have taken teams annually from the United Kingdom for short periods of time to work with the charity 'TransformAsia' in Cambodia. Edwin has also helped to establish a United Kingdom based health charity, 'Transform Healthcare Cambodia,' which sends teams of clinicians to help, support and train Cambodian colleagues, in aspects of health care.

Edwin was a professor and medical consultant and previously a Director of Public Health in the United Kingdom.

In addition to Cambodia, during the early unstable days of the Rwandan genocide, in 1994, Edwin led a team to provide emergency aid and services to the displaced people spilling into the former French Congo.

Through his humanitarian work with refugees and displaced people in war zones Edwin has a 'first-hand' understanding of the human cost of conflict.

He has sought to highlight the need for us all to understand the suffering of individuals within the context of war, including the need for peace and reconciliation to heal those affected and help rebuild their lives and communities.

Prologue

A Walk in the Silence

Have you ever come across someone in your life who is remarkable? Truly remarkable? Someone who through their life has made you question the value of what you are doing and why? Someone whose life challenges your own way of thinking, saying and doing? In essence, your purpose for your time on this earth. This book is about such a challenging confrontation.

I first met Bob when working with Khmer refugees on the Thai-Cambodian border in 1989. There was nothing remarkable in his general physique, though his ginger hair, beard and purposeful blue eyes, were in contrast to the black hair, whisker-less chins and dark brown eyes of the Khmer people we were helping. I confess I thought Bob was a little scruffy – by middle class 'western' standards. His well worn jeans and t-shirt had seen better days. How judgemental and superficial I could be.

Bob, I learnt, was a Brother in the order of Jesuits. He had committed his life to poverty, chastity and obedience (to his Lord, Jesus Christ). For those who are not religiously inclined this may sound absurd. For those who do hold a strong faith it can still be difficult to believe. I found it a hard concept and wondered if Bob could be truly faithful to his 'calling'.

25 years later I can say with absolute certainty that Bob has been true to his calling, living and serving the poorest of the poor. In those 25 years Bob has dedicated his life to being with Khmer refugees as they eked out an existence in war-torn refugee camps. He campaigned for them selflessly through non-violent action, fighting for peace and reconciliation of the fragmented Khmer people and their warring factions. He lived as one with them during their returning to war-ravaged Cambodia. He has been constantly with the poor, sharing in the suffering and joys of their lives. He remains with them even now and continues to fight for them. 'Blessed are the peacemakers' (Matthew 5:9), and Bob is one for sure.

This book is a select collection of short true tales from 'the life of Bob'. He penned them between 1984 and 2006. Bob is a reflective writer and these short vignettes are from his diary and writings. They include his eye witness accounts.

Bob has been involved with Cambodian people since 1979. For ten years he worked in various Cambodian guerrilla and refugee camps along the Thai-Cambodian border. He became protection officer for one of the large refugee camps. He trained as a physician's assistant and coordinated a tuberculosis treatment programme. Bob continues to live, work among and 'walk' with the poor of Cambodia. His heart and life are with the Cambodian people. He works tirelessly for peace and reconciliation, offering his expertise in conflict resolution and active non violence.

I was honoured when Bob asked me to keep his documents and gave me permission to use them as I saw best, not for him, but for the 'poor', particularly the Khmer people. They have been in my attic for almost ten years *(I need to confess this to Bob the next time I see him)*. Following a visit to Cambodia in November 2014, where I was reunited with Bob, I believe it is now right to share these profound writings. If you are someone with a compassionate spirit they will speak to you. If someone seeking justice in the world, they will speak to you. If someone comfortably happy in their current lifestyle but beginning to question, 'what's it all about' they may speak to you too.

In the last 25 years Bob has always walked, literally and spiritually. He strides out daily among the people and places; always to be with the poor. If anyone has spiritually gone the second mile, then he has exceeded this, by far. He has found walking to be part of his life-long vocation and calling. Walking is his tool rather than talking. Doing rather than speaking! Bob likes to walk and meditate, to listen to and be in the presence of God. He describes this as a 'walk in the silence', the silence that is being with God.

Finally, again I need to be clear in respect to Bob; this book is not about him! That would be the last thing he would want or agree to. The book is about situations in the world that should not be tolerated. I hope these personal tales and reflections can inspire the reader, whoever you may be, to be a peacemaker. We cannot be 'Bob' but we can learn from his selfless service of love to others.

It's a remarkable lesson.

Edwin Pugh March 2015

Some

Some stood up once, and sat down.
Some walked a mile, and walked away.

Some stood up twice, then sat down.
'It's too much,' they cried.
Some walked two miles, then walked away.
'I've had it,' they cried,

Some stood and stood and stood.
They were taken for fools,
they were taken for being taken in.

Some walked and walked and walked –
they walked the earth,
they walked the waters,
they walked the air.

'Why do you stand?' they were asked, and
'Why do you walk?'

'Because of the children,' they said, and
'Because of the heart, and
'Because of the bread,'

'Because the cause is
the heart's beat, and
the children born, and
the risen bread.'

Daniel Berrigan*

*Daniel J. Berrigan (b. 1921), is a peace activist and poet. He joined the
Jesuits in 1939 and was ordained to the priesthood in 1952. This poem, loved
by Bob, gives an insight into Bob's vocation among the poor.

Part One: Personal Tales

Hell Broke Loose at Christmas 1
Introduction by Edwin Pugh

A genocidal dictator, Pol Pot, seized power in Cambodia on the 17th April 1975 and with his Khmer Rouge army, ruled until their overthrow on the 7th January 1979. The entire country of Cambodia was turned into a slave labour camp. Man's inhumanity to man was displayed at its best. In this inhuman world, people were dehumanised. Families were separated. Names abolished. Speaking forbidden. Dignity destroyed. Trust annihilated.

It is estimated that the Khmer Rouge policies resulted in the deaths of 1.7 to 2.5 million people out of a population of 8 million. Starvation and disease were major killers as people were exposed to the elements, made to labour 18 hours a day and forced to live on less than subsistence levels of food. The large numbers dying or killed under the Khmer Rouge were buried in mass graves. These sites became known as the 'Killing Fields'. Analysis of 20,000 mass graves revealed at least 1.3 million victims were executed.

Many people tried to escape and flee from Cambodia. Many died trying. But better to try than exist in their current world of Hell. Many battled through fatigue, famine, jungle and landmine-infested undergrowth to reach neighbouring Thailand. Here refugee camps were established along the Thai-Cambodian border to cater for the tens of thousands of people fleeing the atrocities of their homeland.

Camps were meant to be a sanctuary. Although, theoretically, for civilians they also became the sanctuary of soldiers of the various warring factions. After all, here the soldiers got protection, food and healthcare. Camps became 'legitimate' military targets and shelling became a regular occurrence for the refugees.

Despite the Khmer Rouge being defeated in 1979 the camps remained and developed a life of their own. Many Cambodian refugees, unable to return home, found themselves imprisoned and totally dependent on external aid for another 10 years within the wire-walls of the camps until their eventual repatriation. The legacy of the Khmer Rouge years and the border camps pervades and influences the country and touches the lives of people in Cambodia to this day.

What follows is an abridged factual account taken from a report written by Bob for the United Nations Border Relief Operation about an incident that occurred in the refugee camp of Nong Samet over Christmas-time 1984. Nong Samet camp was located just inside the Cambodian border. Over 60,000 refugees were housed there.

This true story follows the patients being treated for tuberculosis and their families who were forced to flee Nong Samet as it came under a major attack from the Vietnamese on Christmas day 1984. It is estimated 10,000 shells fell on Nong Samet. Bob was the coordinator for the tuberculosis service at Nong Samet and was with the refugees during this traumatic time. The patients and staff were personally known to him.

He wrote the report.

In-patients and Staff of Tuberculosis Clinic in Nong Samet Refugee Camp - December 1984.

Mom Seay - In-patient with 17 year old son, Mok

Leang Lorn - In-patient with wife and 2 year old daughter

Luong Boy - In-patient with daughter, Khoum

Ouk Khom - In-patient with wife

Soth Sour - In-patient, health worker and night guard

Sok Sopal - Tuberculosis clinic supervisor

Bob Maat - Tuberculosis service coordinator

Thang Chhoy - Head nurse

Sok Heng - Trainee laboratory technician

Hell Broke Loose at Christmas 2

A Normal Day:

Monday, December 24th 1984 was a 'normal' day at the tuberculosis clinic in Nong Samet refugee camp. One hundred and fourteen patients came as usual for their medicines.

This Monday five people were being treated as in-patients at the tuberculosis clinic. Mom Seay, a somewhat cantankerous old woman, was yelling at her youngest son Mok, a 17 year old boy, who was the only family member who hadn't abandoned her. One could feel sympathy for both sides of that family argument. She was partially blind from cataracts now and unable to walk without assistance due to an old back injury from the Pol Pot days. Because of these physical and social problems Mom Seay had become a long standing resident of the tuberculosis clinic.

Leang Lorn, a 37 year old gentleman, stayed with his wife and two year old daughter. He had begun treatment two months ago for his lung disease but after one month of treatment he suffered a severe allergic hypersensitivity reaction. By the 24th December he was still weak but the fevers had subsided. His appetite was back to near normal but he was quite jaundiced. He spent most of the day scratching and picking off the dead skin left behind by his dermatitis caused by the allergic reaction.

Three months earlier Luong Boy, a 63 year old man, had arrived from the Cambodian city of Battambang with his only daughter, Khoum. He was in severe respiratory distress upon arrival at the hospital. He had fluid drained from his lungs with temporary relief of his shortness of breath but the fluid continued to recur. But now Luong Boy and the medics were concerned about malignancy as he showed little improvement on treatment. The medics had discussed with Luong Boy, before beginning therapy, about the likelihood of him having lung cancer also. The option of his going back to his village near the city of Battambang was discussed so he could be close to home if he had to die. After a day to think it over he said he wanted to live or die in Nong Samet. By the 24th he still was unable to walk to the latrines nearby without assistance. His daughter took care of most of his needs.

The fourth patient was a 58 year old gentleman named Ouk Khom. He had been admitted several days earlier from Nong Samet's hospital with pneumonia. He looked older than his years and was somewhat confused. His wife, a very strong, well nourished woman, seemed to be the one in charge. On the afternoon of the 24th he told the medics he didn't want to be treated. It was unclear why he was confused. Was it because of his age as his wife insisted? Was the confusion a sign of tuberculosis infection of the brain? Or could it be the Khmer way of expressing anger towards one's wife? With the latter being felt to be the real cause of his 'confusion' he was told he could be discharged in the morning if he wanted, but, maybe he should discuss it with his wife once again in the evening.

Lastly there was Soth Sour, a quiet, but friendly 25 year old man who lived at the tuberculosis clinic. He would complete treatment for his tuberculosis in four days. For the past two months he had become the tuberculosis clinic guard by night and a health worker by day. Living at the tuberculosis clinic he was available most of the time for any problems that might occur.

It was a routine day for the tuberculosis clinic staff. Sok Sophal, the supervisor had the day off. He had arrived in Nong Samet almost one year earlier from the capital of Cambodia, Phnom Penh, where he had been in medical school for two years. He stopped by the clinic in the afternoon for class. Also, he was discussing the latest rumours on the Vietnamese troops' movements.

Thang Chhouy, the head nurse was busy. He was a quiet sensitive fellow. He knew the border well from his previous market trading days. A fellow trader carried him to Nong Samet in October 1981, after he had already wasted away to 25 kilograms. He was dying of tuberculosis. Since medicines were hard to acquire at that time the tuberculosis coordinator momentarily debated whether he should withhold the medication from Thang Chhuoy and save it to give to those with a better chance of survival. Needless to say Thang Chhuoy won that debate and now was a solid 35 kilograms minus one lung. Over the years he graduated from being a helping hand to health worker to nurse. Now he was 'head nurse', even if the only nurse, at the clinic. Thang Chhuoy was also the keeper of the medicines. He kept five days worth of medications for the tuberculosis patients hidden in his house in case of emergency.

The last permanent member of the team was Sok Heng, a thin, gaunt looking fellow from the city of Battambang. In 1983 he had been treated for tuberculosis for eight months in Battambang. Publicly he'd tell you he stopped treatment because the medic at Battambang city's tuberculosis hospital told him he was cured. Privately, he admitted he stopped treatment prematurely because he felt so much better. Four months after he stopped his therapy he coughed up blood. Tests revealed active disease. Showing no improvement after four months of re-treatment he came to Nong Samet. He had subsequently been treated for six months at Nong Samet for what was felt to be probable resistant tuberculosis (resistant to usual medicine combinations). He was learning the staining and reading of laboratory slides used to diagnose tuberculosis. He would hopefully become the permanent tuberculosis laboratory technician with a little time and experience. The 24th ended with class for the whole tuberculosis staff.

Christmas Day 1984

At 5.25am Soth Sour said he heard the first shells fall inside the camp. He had been hearing the movement of tanks since 3am. With the sound of those first explosions the patients were already beginning to gather their belongings. Luong Boy's daughter had already gone off in the early morning to gather grass from the fields leaving him alone. Mok, Mom Seay's son, picked up the old lady and carried her on his back as she yelled orders to him all along the way. Ouk Khom's wife got her husband up - no time to put on clothes - dressed only in his sarong she walked him down the road amongst the crowd. Leang Lorn's wife tried to hold up her husband with her left arm, carry their 2 year old daughter on her right arm and their bag of earthly belongings over her right shoulder. Often along the road they would have to stop because Leang Lorn was too weak. Finally he told his wife to put him in the ditch along the side of the road. He urged her to go on without him and take their daughter to safety. His wife, crying, refused and stayed with him until he'd gotten up again. At one point Leang Lorn said he was so thirsty he urinated into his own hands and drank the tea-coloured urine.

All followed the same path - down past the tuberculosis clinic, left turn on to the main road past the hospital, right turn on to the old Samet market road down to the old Buddhist temple. From there, if the attack seemed severe, they would be instructed to proceed down to the Thai strategic canal. Also known as the 'tank ditch' the strategic canal was a large ditch about five meters deep and fifteen meters wide which ran the length of the Thai-Cambodian border. It was built as a deterrent to Vietnamese tanks entering Thailand.

Luong Boy, without his daughter, was very much alone. He could walk only a few feet before getting short of breath. Soth Sour, seeing all the rest of the patients off went back to help the old man. Luong Boy told Soth Sour to leave him and go on alone. Soth Sour refused but Luong Boy wouldn't allow him to stay. Luong Boy told him to help his own family in camp. Soth Sour reluctantly placed him safely in the ditch. Then he ran back to the tuberculosis clinic. He locked the door to the store room and got lost in the panicking mass of people. Later that morning it would be reported that shells had fallen on the tuberculosis clinic.

The population of Nong Samet, some 60,000 people, began to arrive at the strategic canal by 6.30am. The Thai military was all over the place, as well as many news reporters. The Red Cross arrived with their ambulances 30 minutes later. The Thai authorities were holding up the people on the Cambodian side of the strategic canal. There was active heavy shelling less than three kilometers behind the people with clouds of dark smoke billowing up. Nong Samet refugee camp was burning. A good number of the handicapped people were allowed over the ditch and were seated together – those in wheelchairs, some with crutches. A makeshift medical triage area was set up across from the Royal Thai army check point. Some pregnant women in labour were allowed to cross the ditch to the triage area.

By 7.30am the Thai authorities gave permission for the people to cross the ditch to allow them access to a prepared evacuation site about two kilometers north west of their location. Most people carried what belongings they were able to grab in their haste. Many had brought their pigs and chickens with them, but no cattle were seen coming across the ditch. Many came with their bicycles, carrying their elderly or disabled on the backs of the bikes. A few tuberculosis patients arrived at the triage area.

The tuberculosis patients were but a very small minority in the tragedies of the day. The 'ditch scene' continued all morning. The Red Cross was very busy transferring the more severely wounded to Khao I Dang, a neighbouring refuge camp located just inside Thailand. Those needing transportation sat off to one side. They included the elderly, the full term pregnant women, the 'wheel-chairers', the lame and the minor war injured who couldn't walk. A large cargo truck with large red crosses draped over its sides was brought in. The handicapped, including those in wheel chairs, went first. There were a few Khmers just sitting along the road who refused a ride in the truck. They said they were waiting for their Thai friends to help. One of these was Vanna Reth, a 40 year old tuberculosis patient. Vanna Reth was quite a wealthy woman often wearing her gold earrings and rings to the clinic. Even if one had a lot of money in Nong Samet one was usually more discrete. However her wealth came in handy as she paid to get a ride directly to the safety of Khao I Dang.

Another tuberculosis patient, not known to the Nong Samet tuberculosis staff, was having trouble. Chhem Sim, a 38 year old, 75 kilogram woman, rather large by Khmer standards, lived with her 21 year old daughter and her 19 year old son. Her son was a soldier and was at the front at this time. At the beginning of December she began to experience low back pain and numbness in her legs. On December 22nd she became unable to walk and had no control over her bladder function. With the eruption of shelling on Christmas day morning her daughter was unable to move her. When the shelling became more intense the young girl ran. Chhem Sim says she spent most of Christmas day crying. She was alone and helpless in her hut in all the shelling for the next two days until, on the 27th December, a Khmer soldier heard her cries. He got some other soldiers to help. With a hammock and a bamboo pole they carried her to the 'tank ditch' where an ambulance took her to Khao I Dang.

By 11am that Christmas day most of the camp population had crossed the strategic canal. The security coordinator was told to speed up the departure of the last truck carrying refugees. Spotted in the short distance was Ouk Khom being helped along by his wife. His wife shouted, 'Kaught dung khluen howee,' meaning, 'My husband knows himself already'. It seems the Vietnamese attack had shaken him from his confused state of yesterday. Now he wanted to be treated for his tuberculosis. He and his wife were the last people to be put on the truck before it pulled out.

By 11.30am an emergency medical team was allowed into the evacuation site. The hospital, out-patient department and mother and child health clinic people were all beginning to work out of the same bamboo building. The most severely dependent people were taken to the hospital first. Some of the elderly were picked up by their families there. The handicapped people stayed together. Two mothers who gave birth at the 'tank ditch' came with the other dependent patients. The obstetric ward was the first to fill up. One of the last severely poorly patients to arrive was a deceptively healthy looking young man with suspected smoke inhalation. He died about an hour after admission.

The tuberculosis medicines were to be given out at the out-patient department. Soth Sour, the health worker, was the first of three tuberculosis staff to arrive. He related the story of what happened in the tuberculosis clinic on Christmas day morning. He told sadly of his inability to help take Luong Boy to safety. Sok Sophal, the clinic supervisor, showed up a while later. He had been on night duty at the surgical ward. He had been relieved that he had sent his wife and children to Khao I Dang a few weeks earlier using a guide at night time. His wife had been especially afraid of a Vietnamese attack since the Vietnamese attacked another camp in November. Thang Chhuoy, the head nurse, showed up smiling. He had escaped with his wife, his two children and a bicycle. He said he was unable to carry out the extra tuberculosis medicine that he had hidden in his house. It was later learned that the Khmer military had looted his house. Sok Heng, the trainee laboratory technician, didn't come to the hospital but he had been seen alive and well by other members of the team.

Of the one hundred and twelve patients on tuberculosis therapy, seven did not get their treatment on the day of evacuation. In their panic they had left their medicines at home. One patient borrowed his medicine from a fellow patient who was receiving the same dose. The remaining patients had taken their medicines; some before fleeing, some on the road and the majority celebrated they had survived the onslaught by taking their pills at the evacuation site.

Meanwhile Ouk Khom was staying on the adult medicine ward. He was still quite short of breath in the makeshift hospital. It was felt it would be best to send him to the hospital at Khao I Dang. His wife, always in charge, refused to let him go unless she went along. Considering his condition and the perilous security situation he and his wife were sent in the late afternoon to Khao I Dang. He was begun on tuberculosis treatment the next day.

Wednesday December 26th

The entire staff showed up for work the next morning. Two white tents were erected adjacent to the hospital. Half of the second tent was set up for the tuberculosis clinic. For a couple of hours in the afternoon the tuberculosis supervisor and coordinator drove round announcing (through a megaphone) the location of the tuberculosis clinic. By late afternoon nearly all the tuberculosis patients were accounted for. One was known to have been left behind in Nong Samet. Most had attended clinic in the morning and the rest had been seen and assumed to be still taking their 'tnam kapea'. By this time Luong Boy's daughter had received the devastating news that her father was dead; an eyewitness said he saw a dead body in tuberculosis clinic when he ran past it.

Most tuberculosis patients greeted each other as old friends. They laughingly related their horrifying tales of escape from Vietnamese gunners. Some laughed at how a few were afraid the tuberculosis coordinator would be angry at them for losing their pink treatment cards, or having left their 'tnam kapea' behind in their panic. A few of the patients asked to stay that night in the makeshift clinic.

Mok showed up saying his mother, Mom Seay, was alive and well and telling how he carried her out of the tuberculosis clinic. Mok took the tuberculosis coordinator to see his mother since he didn't want to carry her again. Mok led him about a half a kilometre away where they found Mom Seay sitting in a shady spot among many trees. She complained about the dust, no food, too cold last night, too hot now, no mosquito net, no blanket and what was the tuberculosis coordinator going to do about all that? It was obvious after a few minutes that she was happy to be alive to tell her woes. It was agreed that for the next two days, until something could be set up, Mok would come to get the medicines for his mother. The sons of Ouk Khom showed up asking many times (to make sure) if their mother and father had arrived safely in Khao I Dang. Two days later we received news that Ouk Khom's children had joined their parents.

Sok Sophal, the tuberculosis supervisor, had the clinic all set up like before by the end of the second day. Even the 'welcome' signs used at the tuberculosis clinic in Nong Samet, one in English and one in French, with a picture of the 1984 Olympic mascot, were back in place. Last September Sok Sophal had sketched the drawings himself on bright orange cardboard. He had copied the Olympic mascot from an issue of 'Time' magazine announcing the Olympics. The signs became an identifiable marker for the tuberculosis patients in the evacuation site.

Post Script: Thursday December 27th

'Owpuk nek in got town slop ta!' 'Your father's not yet dead!' It wasn't exactly, 'He has risen,' but for Luong Boy's daughter, the early morning messenger's words relieved much grief, suffering and guilt. Her father, whom she felt she had abandoned during the attack and already *(wrongly)* reported dead, had been brought to the tuberculosis clinic early in the morning by the Red Cross. Luong Boy said he spent most of Christmas day in the ditch by the big tree in front of the old tuberculosis clinic. By early evening when it was a bit quieter he struggled to the 'Pet Thom', (big hospital), where there were more people around. The first night he was afraid the hospital would be a target so he slept outside. On the 26th he was taken inside the hospital and spent a day and a night there. Early on the 27th some soldiers carried him up to the strategic canal. Since Luong Boy identified himself as a tuberculosis patient he was brought to the tuberculosis clinic. That night Luong Boy and his daughter slept together in the tuberculosis clinic.

Even The Crazy Man Wept

A particular incident that took place during an emergency evacuation of the refugees from Nong Samet Refugee camp to a place of safety.

The move did not go smoothly. It was nobody's fault really or maybe it was everyone's fault. The Khmer administration had it all well planned. Nong Samet camp was organised into 13 'quarters'. Within the quarters were groups of houses known as, 'ilots'. Folks in each quarter of the camp knew what day it would leave. Two or three buses to a cargo truck was to be the method. There were a number of 'loading dock' areas for the people living in the quarters to depart from. The quarters leaders became traffic and crowd controllers to a nearly impossible task. Using megaphones, the quarters leaders workers called out the 'ilot' and groups that were leaving next. Three buses pulled up to the loading site along with a cargo truck. People threw all their belongings onto the truck, and then rushed into the buses.

It differed by quarter but moving seemed to occur in various degrees of controlled versus uncontrolled mob rule. Chaos seemed to be the mood of the day. The three-buses-to-a-cargo-truck formula broke down early on as the bus drivers were anxious to get on the road. Since they were being paid by the trip, they were apparently not very concerned about waiting for the cargo truck or other buses. The fact that people had to look for and find their belongings on 'their' cargo truck, well, that would be a problem for the people on the other side. People who had sat around calmly, laughing and joking as they waited, seemed to go in a frenzy the moment the buses arrived in their location. Having thrown their possessions, willy-nilly, onto the cargo truck they rushed the buses. Old people were pushed aside and knocked down, while children were walked over in the mad rush to get on the buses. Children and dogs were passed through the windows of a bus only to be tossed out the other side of the bus by some irate passengers. Families were separated. It seemed Darwin's theory, 'the survival of the fittest,' was being put to the test. It would have been more understandable if, as on Christmas day, they were running for their lives. But these two days were relatively quiet with only occasional shelling in the distance. The behaviour might have been more understandable if they were sneaking into Khao I Dang at night but this was a Thai-permitted, free, day trip to a safe location right next to Khao I Dang. Maybe they were afraid there would not be enough buses or that the Thai authorities and the United Nations Border Relief Operation officials would leave them behind. Maybe they did not know that the new site would be more of a prison for them than a paradise. For those who had the privileged status of being observers it was sad; it made one a little sad to be human; sad, not in a judgemental sort of way, but sad as a reflection on us human beings. Maybe they had been through too much. Whatever the excuses, humankind did not show its best side during the move.

It became clear the move would be completed by mid-afternoon. Though everything had not occurred exactly as planned, at least things happened at a quicker pace than scheduled. The very last civilian group to leave was from quarter 13. By radio they were told they would have to wait another 20 to 30 minutes until the next bus arrived from Khao I Dang. There were about 25 people all together. They had sent their belongings on the last cargo truck. As they sat in the dust some contemplated the Khmers' sad fate while others wondered out loud if they would ever see their possessions again ('Barang, what was the number on that last truck?').

Suddenly, a young man shouted, 'Manu chakuit, pto nah?' (*The crazy man, where is he going?*). A few hundred metres away there was a man dressed only in a towel. He was covered in mud as if it had been pasted on his body. He was sitting in a pile of human excrement, drinking mud water out of a bottle. The stresses of the last few days had been tough on everyone. But, if one was already psychologically borderline, these days were enough to send you over the edge.

In his present state no one recognised him. As the bus pulled up people knew they could not leave him alone in the rubble. Three men went out and got the 'manu chakuit' and carried him to the bus. He fought, kicked and screamed all the way. His towel fell off in the struggle so the men placed the now-naked man on the bus. It was clear from the beginning this would not work out very well. As the bus passed the administration building it stopped at the Khmer Women's Association which was just packing up. The United Nations Border Relief Operation's contact person for the Khmer Women's Association was there. She recognised Sotear, the 'manu chakuit'.

Sotear was well-known to most everyone who worked in the hospital. The medics said the barang *(foreign)* doctors diagnosed him as a paranoid schizophrenic. Those who knew his story well said he had worked in the agriculture department during President Lon Nol's regime. He was an educated man and spoke English and French. It was said he had been 'okay' until 1982 when he got caught in the crossfire during a battle. Ever since then he had been a broken man. His latest home in Nong Samet had been in the Operation Handicap International building. The Operation Handicap International workers had taken him in. They were all wounded themselves, some by polio, some by landmines. To them Sotear was like them, only his wounds were in his head. Sotear never said much; maybe it was the drugs that kept him quiet, but he worked, ate and slept right alongside them in the workshop. The events of December 25th, the day of the attack, had changed the only stable environment that he had. Now, for him, as it was written in the myth of Sisyphus, 'the stone was at the bottom of the hill again'.

The immediate question was one of what to do. The United Nations Border Relief Operation's official knew it would be a long ride for all if Sotear was forced to stay on the bus. She asked the security coordinator if he would be willing to take the man in his car over to the neighbouring refugee camp of Khao I Dang. They debated over where exactly to take him. The hospital was difficult because in the past when he was taken there he became quite aggressive with the female patients. Operation Handicap International would not be setting up shop again for a while. It was decided to make a donation to the monks to care for him.

As the last bus pulled out Sotear was left sitting in the dust with his bottle of water. Sotear was placed in the back of the security co-ordinator's Nissan vehicle. Two workers from administration rode with the security coordinator in case Sotear got aggressive and wanted to jump out of the car. Sitting in the car the crazy man did not look so good, covered in mud and excrement. In the meantime someone had found a pair of jeans left over from a donated clothing distribution of a few days earlier. Even though they were a few sizes too big the pants were put on him. He did not smell so good either but a bath would have to wait until he got to the monks.

As they left the administration they drove past a fire that had started in a few abandoned shelters across the street from the hospital. Someone joked that the television and newspaper journalists had started it so they could get one last photo opportunity for their respective news agencies. They really did not need any staged events. The events of the last few days had been enough without any artificial flavouring.

As the Nissan approached the Khmer military check point the military representatives took a quick look at the 'manu chakuit' and waved the vehicle through. Sotear would not have to worry about being drafted into the army ever again, at least not in his present condition anyway. Over the three day move many young men had tried to sneak past the check point. Some tried to hide on top of the buses. Others hid under the baggage in the cargo trucks. One would occasionally see a hand come out from the bottom of the heap trying to secure an airway or relieve the pressure of shifting baggage. No one questioned if Sotear was 'faking it'.

The last check point belonged to the Thai Task Force but they had already gone. As the Nissan turned left, heading towards Khao I Dang, Sotear broke into uncontrollable sobs; the tears rolled down his muddy cheeks. The Khmers in the car tried to console him but to no avail. They told him they were taking him to a safer place, to a place where they would have medicine to cure him.

Maybe the events of the past month have been too much. Maybe it was the insanity of war. Maybe it was the destructive behaviour of what people do to each other to survive. Maybe just the tremendous sadness of the whole border scene was such that, 'even the crazy man wept'.

The Landmine that Grandpa Planted

'I remember hearing an explosion and flying up into the air. When I hit the ground, I looked to my right and saw one of my feet. Looking down at my left leg I saw that foot just dangling', Suwin told me.

'Then what did you do?' I asked.

'I laughed.' He looked at me incredulously. 'Of course, what else could I do but laugh?!'

They say grief leaves the face of the Cambodian quickly but goes down to the heart and stays there a long time. Suwin was twenty-five years old at the time. He's my brother, the second son of the farmer family who adopted me as 'Kon', as a son. I have lived with this family of seven for over ten years. Mother is Cambodian. Father is Thai. They married about 30 years ago on the Thai side of the mobile Thai-Cambodia border markers. The common language of our border village was Cambodian though the villagers were Thai nationals. They too know the war.

Suwin hit his mine along the Thai-Cambodian border in July 1981. His wedding ceremony arranged by the couple's parents, scheduled for December that year, was called off as soon as word of what had happened spread through the village. For what does one do with a legless rice farmer?

Landmines have become the curse of his mother's country. In the early 1980's when I worked in Cambodian refugee camps the people would tell us, 'You will know the Cambodian of the future, for he has but one leg.' It's 1994 now and that damning prophecy is coming true daily. 1 out of every 236 Cambodians has one leg or none, one hand or handless, one eye or totally blind. That's the highest proportion of landmine victims in the world. Angola is 'number two' where 1 out of every 470 Angolans has had part of their body ripped away or their life taken by a land mine.

During most of the 1980's, in addition to medical work in the guerrilla camps, I was security officer for the United Nations supported camps. While it was mainly a job to protect relief workers when the shelling started, it gave me an opportunity to be 'the first one in' and 'the last one out' of the camps daily.

Over the years I took literally hundreds of Cambodians, sometimes two at a time, in the back of a pick-up truck from the camps to the nearest Red Cross hospital, just inside Thailand. We would hear an explosion at the end of a day and wait. Hoping it was 'only' a water buffalo or dog - until the victim was carried in 'sick in stick' *(this was a term used to describe the Cambodian ambulance - two men carrying the wounded in a hammock on a wooden pole).*

In Cambodia today *(1994)* it is estimated that there are 10 million landmines in the ground. Cambodia has more mines than human beings. Who gave the mines? Who supplied the parts? Who didn't over the years? Since the 1960's the French, the Americans, the Soviets, the Chinese and the Thais planted them along their borders, the Vietnamese on theirs. Singapore and Malaysia provide as many as money can buy; and all Cambodian factions have been planting them too. If I am a Cambodian soldier and place a mine in the ground today, my grand-daughter thirty years from now could walk on that mine that grandpa planted.

They say mines are not meant to kill you, only to maim. Actually it is the selling point found in the package insert of a mine being manufactured in Pakistan. 'Operating research has shown that it is better to disable the enemy than to kill him'. However the children don't often survive the blast.

They say mines don't discriminate. True in that it can be the footstep of a soldier, the leg of an old woman gathering wood to cook her family's rice, the hand of a young boy who thought he was catching 'only' a frog, *(one small plastic mine floats in the water - the Cambodians call it 'Heeng', the word for frog)* or the hands and face of a de-miner. But if you are poor and can't afford to pay for health care you usually don't make it. The Red Cross estimates that for every villager who makes it to a hospital in Cambodia two die en route or in the fields. In Rattanak Mondol, a small district in the province in which I now live, forty people 'hit' mines between June and October of this year. More than half did not survive the blast. World-wide they say every hour of every day someone is walking on a landmine somewhere in the world. Of which, most importantly, the victims are human beings whom other human beings loved and needed - whole.

Even The Crazy Man Wept

My brother Suwin is better now. Thailand, a country well down the road to development, has provided him with two good plastic prostheses. He can walk again, but only in the dry as he is unable to negotiate the mud of the rainy season. We often joke how he taught his crazy foreign brother how to plant rice, bring in the harvest while drinking rice wine, catch frogs in the first midnight downpour of the rainy season, be a good water buffalo boy while catching lizards for dinner at the same time - all those things which helped make us brothers; that, as brothers, we will never do together again.

The Mindless Menace of Violence

Beatings, 572; knifings or axing, 185

Suicides, 130; armed robberies, 129

Injuries from mines or shelling, 52

Rape or sexual harassment cases, 48

These were the numbers of episodes of violence reported to the refugee protection unit in 1988.

The numbers do not speak directly to the names and faces that they represent. The numbers do not recount the story of the 'Flying Noodle' man, a well known cook in one of 'Site Two's' refugee camp restaurants, who got into a fatal axe duel with his childhood friend of forty years after their children got into a spat. The numbers cannot graphically display the discovery of a crying two year old girl on a bamboo bed next to her mother, axed to death, and her father, hung to death - all because her father planted his vegetable garden outside his allotted parcel of land much to the consternation of his neighbours - the accused murderers.

The statistics do hide the scars of literally hundreds of battered and abused wives for whom there is no protection other than running to another part of the camp until the husband once again discovers her and drags her home. The statistics do hide the thousand of Khmers who suffered physical and psychological abuse by the Thai protectorate, who not only threatened but fulfilled their promises of worse retribution if the insult done to the victim was made known to the international protection staff. Nor do the numbers show the looks on the faces of the victims who were brave enough to seek out the single Protection Officer discretely to inform him about the abuse inflicted by Task Force 80, a special unit of the Royal Thai army charged with refugee management, only to be told by a representative of the United Nations to 'wait' and 'hang on'. Curves on a graph do not reveal the eyes and the lines in those same faces who after nine long hot dry seasons of Task

Force 80 abuse cried out to the Protection Officer, 'Why? We can't wait!' before walking away sadly with a sense of being betrayed.

The statistics do not televise the masses of poor people, following the advice of United Nations Border Relief Organisation's deputy field coordinator, carrying nightly all their earthly belongings in the early evening to the western fence in the camp as this was the only form of protection from the shells that threatened to fall in the night. At the same time graphs don't hear the queries of those fence sleepers wondering if maybe the United Nations High Commission for Refugees might offer a better safe haven than the western fence.

Statistics tell one important part of the reality. The faces tell another. Over the years the numbers have long claimed there is an 'ongoing and unremitting' problem here. The faces say, well if the numbers ain't clear enough for you, then the very stones will cry out. The faces explain why the Director of the United Nations Border Relief Operation, Y. Y. Kim could speak with such urgency to the world community that the costs of continuing the status quo, 'Are far too high to be ignored'. The faces do bear the price of this mindless menace of violence. After ten years in United Nations supported structures the faces have experienced what the criminal psychologists have taught us; violence breeds violence, repression brings retaliation.

Most of all the faces show the victims of this violence are human beings whom other human beings loved and needed. No one, in any of the camps along this entire border, can be certain who will suffer next from some senseless act of bloodshed. Khmer administrators have been saying 'My people are going crazy'. 'If no settlement soon I will lose control over my people'. Voluntary agency workers have been asked by their Khmer colleagues, 'What is happening to us?' A woman who had overdosed on drugs when asked by the Protection Officer what could be done for her, answered, 'Get me out of here'.

The victims of this violence are rich and poor, young and old, well known administrators and 'unknown' farmers, Thai and Khmer, Vietnamese and Barang *(the foreigners)*. Experts of every shape and sort (health, mental health, security, vocational, United Nations Border Relief Operation, World Health Organisation, United Nations High Commission for Refugees, and International Committee of the Red Cross) have been called in to study the violence. Some speak of time bombs with short fuses; others talk of structural changes and durable solutions. Some look for scapegoats. Most wear rose tinted glasses. Yet this much is clear, the vicious cycle of violence goes on and on and on in an ever upward spiral.

There is another type of violence that the statisticians cannot measure. It is a type of violence, slower but just as deadly, destructive as the shot or the grenade in the night. This is the violence of institutions: indifference and inaction and slow decay. This is the slow destruction of a child by hunger; and schools without books and camps which are only 'marking time'. This is the violence of living in prison-like encampments for much too long; the violence of a decade of dependency.

This is the breaking of a man's spirit by denying him the chance to stand as a father and as a man among other men. This is the degrading of a woman's spirit by denying her the right to stand as a mother and a woman among other women. This is the destruction of an adolescent's spirit by denying him or her the opportunity to grow up as any other child without fences. Indeed it is the violence of spending ones entire life in a community of confinement.

It is the type of violence that blames those caught in its vortex *(the Khmers)* for being victimised. It is the type of violence that can blame those outside its vortex *(the United Nations member governments)* for being indifferent to the fact that our lives on this planet are too short and the work to be done too great to continue to perpetuate the structures that allow this spirit to flourish along this border. And this too afflicts us all.

No simple set of remedies can confront this type of violence that the statisticians, the experts, the names and faces have told us for the past ten years. Maybe ultimately the question is not what programmes we should seek to enact, for we have been enacting programs for ten years in the camps. The question is whether we can find in our midst and in our own hearts that leadership of human purpose that will recognise the terrible truths of our existence at this border.

Speaking to the problem of racial violence in the United States after the murder of his friend and contemporary, Martin Luther King Jnr, a civil rights leader, Robert Kennedy, the brother of the late US President said, 'Of course we cannot vanquish it with a program, nor with a resolution'. 'But we can perhaps remember- even if only for a time - that those who live with us are our brothers *(& sisters)*, that they share with us the same short movement of life; that they seek as we, nothing but the chance to live out their lives in purpose and happiness, winning what satisfaction and fulfilment they can'. Surely, this bond of common faith, this bond of common goal, can begin to teach us something. Surely, we can learn, at least, to look at those around us as fellow men, and surely we can begin to work a little harder to bind up the wounds among us and to become in our hearts brothers and countrymen once again'.

The statistics on the border for 1988 are grim. By all indications the situation is getting worse. If one faces the evils of this border daily and sees what it has done and is doing in an ongoing and unremitting manner, as the people involved directly in protection duties are confronted with, one cannot avoid touching and sometimes being overwhelmed by that 'overwhelmingly - searingly, sad sadness'. I am convinced that specific reality needs to be faced and felt particularly by those in authority who can effect change. Unless early on one, touches that sadness, one doesn't move with that painful honesty, that urgency to act so as to advocate for the truly overwhelmed ones to give them some options out of this deadening environment of the border. Honesty, urgency and advocacy are necessary elements to form that leadership of human purpose to give people a choice.

This is the touch stone for action.

He Calls Me......Christ?

It was in the small village of Kralaam Plook in Battambang province that I
first recall it happened publicly. It was that first Dhammayietra in 1992 in
Cambodia; a walk of peace, of reconciliation, of coming home. 'Years of
violence have brought tragedy', he said. 'More violence will only bring more
harm'.

The marchers, many of whom were returning refugees from the Thai border
camps, travelled about twenty kilometres a day. Each night the
Dhammayietra stayed in a different temple, in another village. This walk took
thirty days and thirty nights from Poipet, a town on the Thai-Cambodian
border, to Phnom Penh, the capital of the country. 'Now', the Joyful
Proclaimer told us, 'is the time for peace'.

Often the marchers would be led to the temple grounds by the local villagers.
Only the remains of a Buddhist Wat would be visible. Yet another temple
without walls, destroyed in the war. But then under a tree one would see a
smiling Buddha statue. Perhaps an arm had been blown off or an ear shot
away by a soldier of an earlier day. 'The suffering of Cambodia has been
deep', he would preach to the villagers gathered at the foot of their broken
Buddha. 'But from this suffering comes great compassion. Great compassion
makes a peaceful heart'.

This was not the first Dhammayietra in history. Indeed the original
Dhammayietra occurred over 2500 years ago in western India. Buddha
himself would take his nuns, monks and lay people on a meditative walk to an
area of conflict, spreading a message of peace. 'Peacemaking is our life', this
Ghandi of Cambodia proclaimed in every village. 'Every step is a prayer.
Every step is a meditation. Every step will build a bridge'.

The second Dhammayietra was a walk from Angkor Wat, the famous temple
in Siem Reap and spiritual centre of Cambodia to the capital Phnom Penh. It
occurred just prior to the United Nations sponsored elections in the country
in May 1993. There had been great fear of violence throughout the
countryside. Prior to the walk he taught the participants, 'We must find the

courage to leave our temples and enter the temple of human experience; temples that are filled with human suffering'.

The walk began on a violent note. As the marchers were assembling at Wat Damnak, it became a battle ground in an early morning gun battle reportedly between government forces and Khmer Rouge militia. A grenade was tossed into the Sala, the large open air building where the walkers were huddled on the floor. The grenade bounced off the Buddha image and fell at his feet. It didn't explode. Later, smiling, the good monk assured us, 'Buddha saved us'.

It was late one evening on this march when four heavily armed soldiers appeared and demanded to see the leader of the walk. Fearing ill intent another monk was 'chosen' to meet the messengers of the night. When he came out the soldiers put their guns down at his feet and requested, 'Please bless us. So that when we shoot our bullets won't hit anyone. And when they shoot at us, their bullets won't hurt us'. They were blessed. 'Didn't he used to whisper to us, listen closely, peace is growing in Cambodia, slowly, step by step'.

When the march entered Phnom Penh it was a city filled with foreboding. For three days over ten thousand people joined the walkers in the streets of Phnom Penh; leaving their homes and their work places to be with the Dhammayietra. Some in the crowd compared it to Martin Luther King Jnr's 1963 march on Washington. The tension eased; the election took place and ninety percent of the people voted. About ten years ago the great dreamer had been asked when peace would come to Cambodia. He answered 'When Buddhist nuns and monks can walk through the streets of Phnom Penh, meditating for peace. Peace will come to my country'.

The third Dhammayietra when it was announced in February 1994 was to be a walk not only for reconciliation between people but with the land itself. Cambodia is rapidly becoming the land of one-legged people. The popular prophecy of the 1980's, 'You will know the Cambodian of the future for he/she has but one leg', is coming to pass. On this procession to the province of Pailin, the headquarters of the Khmer Rouge, the de-miners would be blessed every day as they are preventing suffering. Each day a Dodhi tree was to be planted, a symbol to confront the problem of deforestation in the countryside, done out of greed and the need to support the war effort. 'If we listen to Buddha, Christ or Gandhi', he reminded us. 'We can do nothing else'.

Each day of every walk, whether at four in the morning or eleven am when the day's walk ended due to the heat, the streets of town and countryside would be lined with people sitting in front of their homes with a bucket of water, candles and incense sticks. As the nuns and monks processed by they would pour water over the person's head praying, 'May you have peace in your heart; may our country have peace'. The old people wept. 'Water is cleansing to our people', the great healer explained. 'You are washing away the suffering of war'.

Dhammayietra three struggled along, however. It wasn't as much the violence without as the fear within which guided the walk's leadership from the beginning. The spirit of a true Dhammayietra was painfully missing. Hadn't he tried to warn the walk's steering committee? 'Every time you fear, you die inside'. Didn't he predict? 'Compassion without wisdom can cause great suffering'.

On that day in April as the walk passed single file through a heavily forested area, it got caught in a cross fire between a Khmer Rouge patrol and the government troops. Unbeknown to many walkers a few heavily armed government soldiers had been allowed to join the front of the march. The trigger was set as both sides erupted in massive shooting like a thunderstorm for twenty minutes. One Buddhist nun and one monk were killed with five others wounded. One of the victims, a 'Look Ta' *(older Buddhist layman)*, was asked at his hospital bed; 'Are you angry at what happened today? Do you want revenge?' The Look Ta responded in the words of the supreme patriarch. 'Hatred never ceases by hatred, but only by love is healed. This is the ancient and eternal law'.

It was in Kralaam Plook that Sunday morning of the first Dhammayietra. He is the venerable Maha Ghosananda, the 'Joyful Proclaimer', the 'Gandhi of Cambodia', the 'Good Monk', the 'Great Dreamer', the 'Great Healer', the 'Supreme Patriarch'. He is a man of fifteen languages although the greatest tongue he speaks is the one of the country people. He was preaching to his people of the Buddha when he stopped and said, 'Oh, I notice that Christ is with us today'. 'Stand up, Christ'.

Being the only Christian representative on this inter-religious pilgrimage and in keeping the myth alive that Jesus was a blue eyed man, I stood up as he was looking at me. Maha Ghosananda went on to list many attributes of the Christ whom he knows and respects. 'Christ can take away the suffering of war'. 'You only have to touch him and you'll be cured'.

Well if you are not into such subtleties as analogies, if your Supreme Patriarch says it and Supreme Patriarch's don't lie, if the Supreme Patriarch says Christ is dwelling amongst you. The rest of the villagers brought their blind grandmothers, their sick infants, 'only to touch the Christ'.

That evening I saw the Venerable quietly. 'Venerable, do you remember what happened today?' He smiled. Not wanting to be too confrontational I said, 'You know when you do that you make me kind of nervous'. He smiled again and said, 'But it is true, Christ'. We proceeded to have a discussion on how all beings have the Buddhist nature in us and all have the Christ nature in us. I smiled and said, 'That is true and beautiful. However, could we keep our divine sparks to ourselves until this walk is over?' He smiled and hasn't to this day.

And he calls me…Christ?

And I call him….Buddha.

A Christmas Story

Through the magic of immigration laws I became an 'illegal alien' in this kingdom of Thailand. Anyway, on Christmas day, my visa expired on December 25th. I no longer enjoyed automatic visa renewal since I did not work for a United Nations sponsored agency.

Being the 'good alien' I am, I got my sore butt *(a thirty five hour train and bus ride from Surin, Thailand to Penang, Malaysia which houses the nearest Thai consulate)* as well as the rest of my bodily parts, out of the kingdom by 6pm, Christmas Eve. However by 10pm, soaking wet it's kind of, 'Hey it's the first time its rained here in two months!' - a local Penangian. 'Ya don't say', says a wet me.

Suffering laryngitis from a raunchy head cold I developed before I began the journey, having heard 'no rooms available, it's Christmas', from the twentieth hotel owner; I wasn't such a pretty sight! At that point I began to rack my brains. 'Now where in the scripture have I heard this', 'There's no room at the inn,' before?

Being befuddled by this, yet another sacred mystery *(don't worry we Catholics got a million of them)*, I stumbled across The Inn. Apparently I had been at this hotel at least once, earlier in the evening. Excuse me, but by this time all cheap Chinese hotels were beginning to look alike. I felt pity, i.e. for me the recipient. The manager offered me a bench in the hall way for the night. I took it!

At that moment I think I realised how ole Joseph felt when he stumbled across the stable on his way to the Thai consulate in Bethlehem *(sorry, maybe I am getting my stories mixed up)*. Although, come to think of it, I think Mary and Joseph got a better deal. I doubt Joseph had to put down $4 Malay dollars for his digs. Plus, a stable with a manger is probably a better place to be if your wife is 'gonna' have a baby. That bench in the hall way was no place to deliver a baby. Nonetheless, one could not help from perceiving, there were a lot of folks tryin' to make babies behind those thin walls this Christmas Eve.

Throughout the night I met the long term stayers at this hotel: Tamil refugees, some Indians who described how they survive by taking on scab labour jobs in this racially discriminating environment and two blind people who bumped into this stranger in their hall way. They, each and everyone, wished me a 'Merry Christmas' on the way to the 'jake', the water closet *(toilet, lavatory)*. I doubt there was a Christian in the crowd. Yet they all said, 'Merry Christmas!'

It was then it came to me. It is exactly in dwellings such as this that the Jesus, whom I have come to know and love, would seek to celebrate the anniversary of his birth. Indeed, the Christ in me, once again a stranger in a strange land, was being taken in and welcomed by folks who were just tryin' to make it in life; like shepherds keeping watch over their flocks by night. Touching that, I fell asleep exceedingly glad!

Part Two: Personal Reflections

Poverty Personified

The 'La Storta' experience refers to a vision Ignatius had at La Storta, an area near Rome. Here, in 1537, he saw Christ carrying his cross with God behind. God asked Christ to accept Ignatius as His servant. Christ accepted Ignatius and asked Him to serve. Jesuits are companions of Ignatius.

When I look back on my life where I have met the Lord most clearly and closely it has been in and among His poor folk. I have met Him on the mountain tops for sure but He has spoken to me most clearly in the valley of His people. I have met Him and He has made my heart just alive in the lower east side of Manhattan, living among the poor and taking care of the dying. When He made His will known about the (*Jesuit*) brotherhood it was in the noisy streets of Berkley, Michigan. I have lived with Him in the streets of Detroit at Holy Trinity, with the men of the avenue. In medical school I lived with Him in the slums of Macon Georgia, caring for the black indigents of Macon County. I lived with Him on 20th Street in Detroit while caring for the dying. He certainly revealed Himself to me in His people called refugees.

My second 'La Storta' experience was in the mountains such as these at El Retiro *(a Jesuit retreat centre in California)*. Then it was the mountains of Lao-Thai border. He spoke to me in the wind as there was that sense today walking around El Retiro. But then I lived with Hmong refugees who were lepers. My retreat experiences during the last four years have been with the very poor Buddhist monks when I slept and ate on the floor of a big open building. Or when I was with the lepers.

For me, poverty has almost become personified. It is a great friend to me. Partly because so many of my friends live in it. You want to be with your friends. And I happen to find my Lord and friend Jesus there.

I want to be His companion, there.

My Eye Have No More Tear

'But sometimes in the middle of the night their wound would open afresh. And suddenly awakened, they would finger its painful edges, they would recover their suffering anew and with it the stricken face of their love.'

Albert Camus, The Plague

You know, sometimes I feel a sadness here. A sadness that hides deep below the surface, that only occasionally one can get a glimpse of. Oh, it rears its ugly head more visibly at times, at times of war.

It cannot hide itself very well at the delivery of a baby born in a ditch on the anniversary of the birth of the Prince of Peace *(Nong Samet, Christmas 1984)*. It does not hide so well in the hovels of an evacuation site. But most of the time it is invisible. But always truly there. Always there quietly below the surface. It hides behind the quick Khmer smile. It lies much, much deeper. At a level no medical programme, no feeding programme or United Nations peace keeping force can touch. A sadness that no monk's gentle persuasion or philosophers eloquence can *'piousiz'e* away for us.

It's an elusive sadness. It defies words. It is only felt, sensed or touched upon. And then only for a few moments. Maybe one needs the eyes to see and the ears to hear. But it does seem to dare the human heart to touch it, the human tongue to speak of it and the human hand to write of it. Maybe we should not try to look at it for it will only incapacitate us. Maybe it is a sadness we must run from so we lose ourselves in teaching programmes, in statistical reports for the United Nations Border Relief Operation, in 'Killing Fields' movies and slide presentations.

This sadness is indeed probably all over the world. It is probably the same sadness that lurked in the burnt out ghettoes of the Bronx, in the brokenness one can touch in the soup kitchens of Oakland and in the spirit that terrorises the dreams of the inhabitants of 'Khmer castle' in Minneapolis. Maybe at this border it is more painfully visible. No, you don't have to touch it but know clearly it will touch you. For indeed, maybe it is part of the brokenness that all of us humans share in.

Oh it is this sadness that can cause the human heart to physically ache. Oh it is this sadness that makes one terribly sad, sad beyond tears. It is the sadness that causes Cambodians to say, 'My eye has no more tear'. A sadness that is deeper than words. It is the sadness that the psychiatrist may begin to tap after five years of therapy. It is the sadness that our deep thinkers and artists have tried to expose for us. Have tried to bring to light lest we get lost in its darkness. Maybe it is that, 'Grief that leaves the face of a Cambodian quickly but goes down to the heart and stays there a long time'. Maybe it is the sadness that that other struggling peoples have nearly despaired in the face of.

Quite simply I am sick of poverty, lynchings, stupid wars and the universal mistreatment of my people and obsessed with a rather desperate desire for a new world for me and my brothers and sisters. Maybe it is the sadness that one cries out about when one feels totally abandoned, that even Jesus uttered, 'My God, My God why have you forsaken me?' Maybe it is a type of sadness that snuffs out hope. It is that sadness which mockingly smiles as we inadequately try to throw words at it.

But then sometimes in the middle of the night, even if the words cannot express it, the sensitive mind and feeling heart on this border can touch it. Just don't ask me to define it. For it is sadness that can only be expressed in 'maybes' and parables. On this border it is that sadness that one begins to touch on when one reflects on the words of the old spiritual song, 'Oh, Abraham, where you gonna run to?' as one walks on the road into Site Two refugee camp.

On this border it is the sadness that one begins to feel when one comes to grips with the realisation of the complexities of the politics that causes these folks to continue to be refugees. The sadness one feels when one realises no one's hands are clean.

On this border it is the sadness one begins to touch when one realises these people are in 'no man's land'. The sadness one witnesses in one's friend as he feels he cannot go home because he has been at the border too long, as he comes to realise Site Two refugee camp is more a prison than a refuge, as he knows that even if he did want to go to a third country no one would accept him.

On this border it is the sadness one feels when one realises there is something terribly wrong out here. Something that leaves people in such a state that they'll never be whole again, be it minus a leg or psychologically broken; a state that is literally eating up one's friends.

It is that dull ache one feels when one realises that even good intentions can contribute to the sadness. As when one asks a five year old girl where does rice come from and all she knows is that it comes home on her mother's head every Tuesday morning from the United Nations rice distribution field. For that is all she has ever known since her birth into refugee-hood. Being witness to, not to mention part of, a process that encourages a proud people to become dependent is deeply disturbing.

It is a sadness one touches on when one recognises that even if there was a peaceful solution to this, 'refugee problem,' people will be walking on landmines for another generation.

It is that sadness which causes one to ache as a pregnant mother with two small toddlers in her arms tells you she attempted to abort this third child because she is afraid she can't carry three children in the wake of yet another early morning attack by the Vietnamese.

It is the sadness that comes to the suffering surface when one cries with the legless 22 year old man who speaks of suicide as he has just come to the awful realisation that no woman will touch him now except out of pity.

It is the sadness that can overwhelm one as one watches one of your most talented medics have a psychotic break when he receives the news that his only relative *(and only ticket out of this hell)* died in Canada.

It is the sadness one must struggle with when one is with a despondent 20 year old young man who has lost two arms and an eye to a mine which he was in the process of making, 'to blow off another's legs'.

It is in that quiet stillness that follows your chief medic's question, 'Do you think we are going to end up like the Palestinian refugees?'

It is this sadness I am trying to share with you, my friends; a sadness that can bring refugee and companion of refugee to the brink of despair at times.

You know, maybe this is a sadness that simple farmers should not have to touch. A sadness that children should not have cloud their clear eyes, that even betrays their smiling 'OK, bye-bye', for things that are not 'OK' and the sadness that will not go away on its own.

But sometimes in the middle of the day one realises maybe it is okay to touch this sadness. One realises maybe it is good to touch this one, not to let it to cause us to despair, though it will make you cry. For maybe only when we face it clearly can we learn what true compassion is. A compassion that allows us to share in the suffering of our fellows even when we cannot change their reality. A compassion that does not allow us to abandon those who are caught in its grasp.

And sometimes in the middle of the day one realises maybe we should not run from this sadness, indeed even if we could. Maybe we should face it head on, struggle with it, ache with it, rage against it, touch it deeply, even respect it but always recognise it clearly.

Maybe, when one touches this sadness fully it will motivate to move with an urgency, the urgency with which one moves when one's friend is dying, the urgency with which one would move when one's self is dying.

This is the sadness that will never easily be overcome but maybe we will be able to trust our philosophers once again when they tell us, 'truth crushed, crushed to earth will rise again'. 'For indeed the arc of the moral universe is long but it bends towards justice'.

For didn't even the one who was overwhelmed by the plague teach us, 'perhaps we cannot prevent this world from being a world in which children suffer, but we can ease the number of suffering children, and if you do not do this, then who will?' Did not even the 'Forsaken One' tell us that he has overcome this sadness? Was it not the Khmers who taught us 'only when the sky is darkest can you see the stars?'

But I must be honest with you. You know sometimes I feel a sadness here - and it causes me to tremble.

Now is the Time

An abridged version of an article written by Bob and published in the Book, 'Back to the Future?', a publication of the Committee for Coordination of Services to Displaced persons in Thailand. It reflects on the ten years of existence of the Border refugee camps and the urgent need for them to close.

In the last act of William Shakespeare's play, King Lear, the good and the bad, the wise and the foolish, the weak and the strong, all die alike and the stage is so littered with corpses that there is nobody left except Edgar to stammer the curtain down as best he can. What he says is this, 'The weight of this sad time we must obey. Speak what we feel, not what we ought to say.'

If one would attempt to chronicle the past ten years of life on the Thai-Cambodian border, one would end up with a tale similar to the reflections Dr Rieux wrote of in his journal during the plague. It too is a story where terrible as well as wonderful things have happened. It's a saga whose promises of peaceful endings seem ever elusive. An account, it would appear, in which nobody's hands are clean. It is an epoch that is not yet finished, whose current chapters speak in terms of civil war. The sadness of the past ten years alone demands an epitaph to be written now. But, for now, one can only record as Dr Rieux did in Albert Camus' book, The Plague.

Dr. Rieux resolved to compile this chronicle, so that he should not be one of those who hold their peace but should bear witness in favour of (the victims); so that some memorial of injustice and outrage done to them might endure. He knew that the tale he had to tell could not be one of a final victory. It could only be the record of what had to be done, and what assuredly would have to be done again in the never ending fight against terror and its relentless onslaughts…by all who, while unable to be saints but refusing to bow down to pestilence, strive their utmost to be healers.

The first 'official' entry in the Border Chronicle, although the origins of the story began long before, would be November 14th, 1979. On that day in Border history at the height of the Cambodian crisis, the General Assembly of the United Nations passed resolution 34/32. The General assembly called for an end to all hostilities in the region. In its call for peace the resolution stated:

1. 'Strongly appeals to all states and national and international humanitarian organisations to render, on an urgent and non-discriminatory basis, humanitarian relief to the civilian population of Kampuchea, including those who have sought refuge in neighbouring countries:'

And the world did just that. It responded to the United Nations' appeal with an urgency. The operation, though never easy, was touted as one of the best humanitarian relief operations the world has ever seen

Ten years later on November 22nd, 1989, Khao I Dang Holding Centre and refugee camp quietly 'celebrated' its tenth anniversary of existence. Over the past decade, lying in the shadow of the Thai-Cambodian border, Khao I Dang has been witness to many a tear shed. Tears of joy and sorrow, tears of hope and despair, tears of acceptance *(of resettlement)* and rejection; tears cried out loud and tears screamed in silence. The Khmer expressions, 'I mingle my tears with yours', as well as, 'My eye have no more tear', are now part of the spirit of Khao I Dang. Khao I Dang's role in Border history has mainly been as a shelter, a refuge from the stormy seas.

Khao I Dang's chronicle would display its role as a gateway for one of the durable solutions - third country resettlement - as proposed by the United Nations High Commissioner for Refugees. Given the politics of the present moment that gateway has been closed. Given the politics of the moment there are whispering words Khao I Dang might become yet another gateway for those Khmers who only desire to go home - voluntary repatriation. Khao I Dang could once again offer a ray of hope for those Khmers who only desire a safe haven from the violent tempest while awaiting the day that the current battlefields will be transformed into market places. But, sadly too, Khao I Dang has been battered about over the years by the winds of politics.

Indeed, if one could just page through, year by year, the diary of this Border for the past ten years one would meet a wide range of characters and players who are the flesh and bones of this drama at the Border. Like Dr. Rieux's journal, the diary would show how the 'pestilences' of this Border do seem 'never ending' and 'relentless' at times as the cost in terms of human suffering soars. The diary would depict a regrettable cyclic repetitiveness to problems seen and concrete solutions offered. In reviewing this decade one would find there have been any number of personalities of all nationalities; good women and men of wisdom, wit, creativity, heart and action who have and are continuing to struggle with the seemingly infinite intricacies and complexities of this political and very human dilemma. Each has in his or her own way, though not tasting the final victory, striven their utmost to be healers, as Camus says. Yet the diary is still not closed and the daily entries speak of increasing violence and civil wars.

As we drift into the second decade of Border history it is important to study, to review, to reflect on what has gone before, as 'new' durable solutions are being actively discussed for the future. Wolfe's Law teaches us that, 'those who don't study the past will repeat its errors'. The ten year perspective of the Border bears that out. Later, Wolfe apparently humbled by the scourges of his time, would make one addition to the Law that bears his name. 'Those who do study the past will find other ways to err'.

One of the more painful lessons of the past that should be carried with us into the future, that should affect our manner of proceeding in the present moment as well as in the days ahead, is the need for urgency. Twenty years ago, Martin Luther King Jnr, a Nobel Peace Prize Winner, rhetorically touched upon the need for urgency when speaking out to the evils of yet another civil war. He declared:

'The tragedy is, there is something in history called, 'Too Late'. There are no more sad words in the English language than, 'Too Late'. Across the world steals the thief of time. There is something that we can refer to as a lost opportunity. Oh, we may plead passionately with time to pause in her passage but time is adamant - and rushes on. Over the bleached bones and crumbled wreckage of many civilisations stand directly the pathetic words, 'Too Late'. There is an invisible book of life that fatefully records our vigilance or our neglect. Omar Kayyam is right. The moving finger writes and having writ moves on...Tomorrow may be too late, the book may close'.

Sadly, Martin Luther King Jnr is right

For those Khmers, Thais and Vietnamese who have died by bullet, artillery shell or landmine; it is too late. They will never go home again.

For those unfortunates who now roam this earth on one leg or two bamboo sticks; it is too late. They will never walk normally again.

For those whom the sadness of this decade has left them psychologically broken and spiritually spent; it is too late. They will never be whole again.

For those young people who were born or who have lived most of their early years in 'communities of confinement'; it is too late. Who can ever give them back their youth?

For those unfortunates who walked through the gateway of Khao I Dang into the 'promised land' of third countries; it is too late. Home will never be home again.

For those Khmer families now divided by civil war; it is too late. The scars of these days will never disappear.

For those United Nations member states, donor countries, humanitarian organisations that unconsciously or willingly played a role in this drama; it is too late. This decade's history cannot be rewritten.

Clearly there have been times in Border history when a moral spark could have ignited a light towards a path of peaceful resolution of this conflict. History has taught us once, at terrible cost, the tragedy of a 'lost opportunity'. Now is the time to ignite the ethical imagination of all players in this drama so that present day politics and policies may serve the moral vision of bringing the suffering of the Khmer people to an end. If we would do this, we would be able to hew out of this decade of despair a stone of hope. If we would do this we would free everyone.

In Tennyson's poem, Ulysses, he makes a quiet plea. 'Come, my friends, 'tis not too late to seek a newer world'. On this border, **Now** is the time.

Do You Love Me?

When they had finished eating, Jesus said to Simon Peter, 'Simon son of John, do you truly love me more than these?'

'Yes Lord', he said, 'you know that I love you'.

Jesus said, 'Feed my lambs'.

Again, Jesus said, 'Simon son of John do you truly love me?'

He answered, 'Yes Lord, you know that I love you'.

Jesus said, 'Take care of my sheep'.

The third time he said to him, 'Simon son of John, do you love me?'

Peter was hurt because Jesus asked him the third time, 'Do you love me? 'He said, Lord, you know all things; you know that I love you'.

Jesus said, 'Feed my sheep'.

Gospel of John Chapter 21, verses 15 -17

You know, Lord, I do feel hurt by the fact that you keep asking me, 'do you love Me?'. I don't deny my humanness and I'm not proud of my failures, where I have not helped you or others when I could have. And I was just as much a victim of that evil situation *(the refugee camp)* but I remember the times I almost died - beat up by Thai soldiers. You didn't ask me 'do you love Me?' then. The times I was trying to make tough decisions to evacuate the camp or not; the times I was up most of the night preparing for the next day. The day I carried the boy who was crushed by a water truck to his parents. Lord, I carried his brains home to his mother - the only son of a widowed mother. You didn't ask me then, 'do you love Me?' The times I just hung around the rehabilitation ward and bull-sh***ed with all the young men who are missing one or two legs. The times I bitched because no one seemed to give a sh*t about people's ashes.

All I am saying, Lord, I ain't asking for any rewards but if you don't believe my words, or you don't trust my heart because it is of mixed motivation, all I can say is look at my daily actions and maybe you can point out the many times where I have failed to show you I loved you; where I turned my back on your little ones. All I can say is yes, that's me too. And this is the only brain and body I got. Ask the crazy man if I love you. He can tell you. Ask Bun Khean if I love you. He can tell you. He worked with me nightly. You knew where my heart was and it was single-minded for, 'Your people'. And when we carried dead babies home in the middle of the night, you didn't ask me anything. And when we walked mothers home from their Calvary, all I could hear was silence, so Lord, don't push me on this, I have a few questions for you too.

And if we are really talking about companionship and friendship on a purely human level, that's a two-way street and I know you as Lord, but that's two ways too, Lord, isn't it? And when the 155mm shells were dropping, and I was scared in the ditch with sixty thousand people, frightened people waiting to come over, I didn't hear you say anything. When we delivered a baby at the ditch, a kid born into war, literally on the anniversary of your birth, at least you had a cave. I didn't hear you ask me anything. I really ain't asking for a pat on the back from anyone. No one but you and me know much of what went on over there.

But, please, Lord, why do you ask me over and over again? Not even the folks over there ask me if I loved them. They knew it. And they probably wouldn't ask in those words anyway. You know how I work and go about my life. I do it quietly. You know I am a quiet lover. You taught me that way. The left hand need not know what the right hand is doing. You taught my mother that way and many things I did quietly or took a hard stand, an unpopular stand or confronted people when it would only make me look bad because I think with you I discerned it was the most loving thing to do. It was the just way. For people were just out and out-lying and I felt the truth must be known. At these times - maybe you did - but I don't remember you asking me, 'do you love me more than these?'

And I am not here to rest on my laurels and I would do it all over again *(and do it better, hopefully)*. I am willing and want to go back but I ain't doing that blindly. I ain't doing it out of some morbid need. From the day I've come to know you, it has been through your suffering people. You have blessed me with many skills and somewhere along the way you taught me to love. So what do you expect me to do when I see a crying need. I know my skills and you've given me this heart. What do you expect? What do you expect me to say when you ask me that again, as you have many times since I've been back, not just in this retreat time.

Don't do that to me. If you want to show me how to love, please I beg you, show me. If you want to show me your heart, and draw me into your heart, your life, let's go. Show me the way. If you want to show me the Father, who is love, the Spirit who is truth please don't wait. Bring me to the point where I can understand. If I need to look at my sin, my failure to understand your greatness, OK, let's go. If my motivation is all screwed up, OK, show me. But please don't question my base-line motivation which is love because you put it there.

It hurts me when you do that.

Now I've said all that, take these as the words of a man who should be asleep. If you question my past loyalties, please don't do that. If you don't believe my word, please believe my past actions when I did try. Know what I did I did because of you. If you are asking me for the here and now, let's go.

This Evil is F*****g Wrong!

The writing that follows reflects the heart of Bob in the anger he feels at the evil that exists in the world and in particular to the people he loves with all his being, the Khmer. In reading it please do not be offended at the language. The swearing is heart-felt and reflects Holy anger. Be offended at the object of the anger – EVIL. God gets the brunt of his anger.

EP

Lord, I really can't find the words. I'm just f*****g tired of the evil that eats up my friends. That leaves people in such a state. That they'll never be made whole again, be it minus a leg or psychologically broken. Or to the point they'll never be happy again because they've lost everything. And think, if you who are God can't do anything about it except talk about kingdoms that aren't of this world, man, what answer is that? Why is evil so f*****g stronger than goodness? And why are so many folk left broken because of it? Lord, I'm still unable to tell You how I really feel.

A friend says these *(refugee)* camps are an abomination against human nature. You mean people can never go home again? Because of politics? Man, I can't write about it. I'm angry, I'm sad. It makes me sick. I'm unhappy, I'm frustrated and you know there is not a damn thing I can do about it and it's been that way since the beginning of time and it's going to be that way till the end of time. Religious folks *'piousize'* it and try to philosophise it away and yet there is no end to the process. Violence breeds violence. There is no peace. So I want to label it evil. And there is no end in sight.

God is calling companions to himself to fight evil, to ease suffering. Yeah, Lord, I'll go. I'll die in the effort. And the suffering will still go on. There'll be one more hero in the fight against evil. It's almost as if the gods can't control evil. Let the little man go and try to control it himself. Because we have no one else we can depend on. It's like people telling Martin Luther King Jnr, wait, wait for segregation to change. It's like God saying, wait, creation is in process. Can't we expect more from a God who is love?

You say, these are man-made policies that have caused these atrocities. Well Lord, what the hell am I supposed to do with that? Chuoy didn't make these policies and he's just trying to be a farmer and he happened to get tuberculosis. He was dying of it so he came to a place where there was a cure. Now he's stuck in no-man's land. He can't go home because he's been at the border too long. He can't go to Thailand because they won't accept him. Even if he wanted to go to a third country he's not eligible. He just wants to go home and meagre out a poor existence. The same existence he would have if there was no war. Lord, that's the evil I'm talking about. Situations to cause the crazy man to go crazy. His was the sanest response out there to that situation. The most appropriate response of an educated man who's lost everything, who shot himself in the leg so he wouldn't have to get caught in the goddam - war, who did everything he could including going nuts in a desperate attempt to get to a third country. And he's been rejected by all.

It's a fifteen year old young woman, dying in a water tank while she was hiding from Thai soldiers who were doing a house to house search for 'illegals'. Illegals to what? To the world? And then her dying in that water tank. That's the evil I'm talking about, man. And that's just one small part of the world. What do you do with that evil? And it ain't going to stop. And if the God of Love is powerless against it, what the hell are the people who give a sh*t supposed to do? What the hell are people supposed to do? We are totally helpless.

I don't know what to do with my anger. I'm angry at me, I'm angry at you, I'm angry at the one who said he'd show me the way if only I'd follow. You, who faced evil from the beginning of time. I don't know what to do. I'm overwhelmed by it all. And Lord, it's like the damn time I got beat up. My response is the same. This is wrong. This is f*****g wrong. Beating up me or beating up somebody else - this is f*****g wrong. And this sh*t is going on daily. It's wrong man, it's f*****g wrong. Whoop, having his eyes burned out, buttons sewn on his skin. It all really happened Lord and its f*****g wrong. And this sh*t is going on daily. It's wrong man, it's f*****g wrong. And Lord, I've seen it. It ain't no magazine article. Yeah, I know life is hard and I know my life has become hardened. What the f**k are you supposed to do? What the hell are we supposed to do with all of this?

Lord, evil scares the sh*t out of me. It is cleverer than I. It can even make me turn against you who I think is the only hope. Because man on his own certainly seems to be f***ed up by it all and can't find his way out. But, Lord, to believe that evil will be overcome is harder to believe than to believe in you, a God who is willing to stand up to evil, a God who has shown he is stronger than evil. But then why don't you finish him off? When you walked this earth you cured evil spirits. When you come into a person's life, 'mountain-top-experience-man' is not afraid. And later he is overwhelmed by the evil one. Why can't you overcome suffering in this world? Why must mankind wait for it in the next?

Because of my anger am I going to change my lifestyle? No. 'Bob, because of our anger, does that mean you don't want to follow me anymore?' No, no, no. But I want you to know Lord I am angry. Angry to the point that I still haven't touched it or said it in words that tap the anger I feel. Or the sadness I feel over it.

And *(yet)* I do feel you are a God who can do something about it.

Silence, the Language of the Gods

The words of this deeply meditative reflection on silence were written by Bob on 10th September 2005. He titled his thoughts, 'Musing in the Silence from the Table Tops of Hoe Peng's Café'. I have taken the liberty of converting Bob's written text into prose. Bob won't mind. The words are the same. And what's more, the silence is the same too.

EP

I would like to walk a little further into the silence.

The silence that is always there,

At our deeper level of consciousness.

It's from that space that I would like to dwell

And view myself, our world,

From that silent space.

The space where I know

You are God.

Given my history in other spaces

I have no name for you.

I don't know what to call you.

The titles of previous names have turned sour on my lips.

I have no name for you, but I know you are there.

No name in the silence.

Dr Edwin Pugh

I would like to go to that space,

Where you view the world.

I will take you there.

There ain't no need for names,

Or titles or words for that matter.

The space you will be when your own tired flesh falls away.

The place where all go when the flesh falls away.

I can take you there; just dwell there.

Let your heart be purified there.

Let your view be clarified there.

I will take you there

For you are already there.

As for my name, I have no name

And am called by all names.

What is a name?

I have no face but I am all faces.

I have no word but I dwell in all words.

I am.

Surely, come into the silence.

I will take you for you are already there.

Even The Crazy Man Wept

The walk continues there.

Breathe in this silence. Sleep in this silence.

Eat in this silence. Walk in this silence

As you live in that world.

Touch both at the same time

Because they exist all the time at the same time.

Listen in this silence. Listen.

Look at the questions of your heart from this silence.

Silence is the last word.

We come from the silence and we return to the silence.

Life and word come out of the silence.

Come into the silence

And know that I am God. You're right,

Whatever that means, whatever that means.

In the silence, from the silence

The world can appear differently.

Make your decisions in the silence

As you walk in the world.

In the silence you can learn

The language of the gods.

Come and listen in the silence.

Come and dwell in the silence.

Live in the silence

As you are loved in the silence.

Let your love come from the silence

From which you came

And to which you will return.

There are no words, no names in the silence.

Dwell quietly in the silence

And see the world.

Let your heart become silent as the silence.

Listen in the silence under any old tree.

In the silence one can hear very clearly.

See very clearly. And no word need be spoken.

Respect this silence.

Be purified in this silence.

The silence that the Buddha sits in.

The silence of no desires.

Go dwell in that silence this day.

Even The Crazy Man Wept

Go find this silence

And begin to let the noises fade away.

Enjoy this world, see this world,

Touch this world, taste this world from that silence.

For that is where you came from,

It is to where you shall return.

It is the silence of the gods.

I Come, I Long, We Fast

I come to you in the quiet of this cold morn. I come to you in the silence of this early morning hour. Tis quiet in this house. Tis quiet in this heart. I wait in receptive silence to hear your voice. A voice which speaks in the quiet silence deep within this one's being.

I long to hear your voice. I long to see your face. I long to touch your presence. I long to be free. I long to be with thee. I long to walk in your step. I long to touch your holiness. I long with expectant heart. I long, even though you said we are never apart.

My strength, my hope, my love, I find in the gods above. I desire that my desires become one with the gods above. One in the silence of the gods above. One in the spirit of the gods above. One in love with the gods above. One in one with the gods above.

This week we try to express in body what the words cannot say. It's a fast in the cold desert. A fast to purify our hearts as our chant tries to purify this human world. It's done with simplicity. It's done with sincerity.

It's done with loving kindness. It's done to confront the blindness that makes us blind. Blind to the suffering we cause one another. Blind to the pain which is done, maybe not out of malice but certainly for self-gain.

Building our dreams on the shattered dreams of others has never been the way of love. In that, no victory is won. Yet we pray for our churches. We care for our young. As we are benefiting from a process that will cause deep, deep suffering, deep pain. It is all being done in our name.

It's being done for our security. It's being done for our gain. It's being done with a blindness to the world's pain. But it is not being done in ignorance or blindness for those in the know. It's being done in arrogance, greed and hatred for the leaders of our land. But they cannot be about it alone. They need our hands. They need our ignorance. They play with our selfish pride and fears.

So we beat a drum with simplicity. We chant a word from ancient times. We fast with our bodies for a world that's out of rhyme. A world that is ignorant of the suffering it has already caused and can cause again. It's for the sins of this world we fast, again and again.

We fast for our friends. We fast for ourselves. We fast for those who have already suffered. We fast to prevent the suffering to come. We fast for the little ones. We fast for a world that increasingly does not want to hear. We fast for we know you are close. You are near. We fast without fear. We fast, come near. We are here.

The Right Road Home

Written at 3am, December 8th 2006, in the Peace Temple, Newport, Tennessee.

Father God, Mother God,

Am I

On the right road home now?

Yes my child,

You are on the right road home.

Sometimes I feel like a motherless child,

Sometimes I feel at home.

Sometimes I feel I could set my feet up.

Sometimes I feel it's time to roam.

Is this place home?

I feel comfortable in your presence here.

I mean I feel at home.

Clearly these sisters and brothers

Are about the work of the spirit.

With them I could be life-long friends.

We've fasted and prayed together.

We've spoken of things of the heart.

Their day to day walk

Is one of peace now.

In your heart they are never apart.

They walk in the city,

They walk on country road.

They walk long distances.

Everyone seems to welcome them

In their homes.

They walk with simplicity.

They walk with spirit.

They beg for what they eat.

They walk with hearts wide open.

They walk with a beat.

They chant with a word of ancient wisdom.

They pray deep in the heart.

They build temples of peace on mountain tops.

On their path of peace.

Even The Crazy Man Wept

They are never apart.

They'd chant all day if they had to,

With song and beat of the drum.

They walk to bring people together.

They walk

So 'we' may become one.

One in a peaceful world,

One in beloved community.

One to end the destruction of all life,

One to end the suffering.

One in setting people free.

They work in the quiet.

They work in the mundane.

They work for peace in the world,

Not for money or fame.

Their teacher is a wise one.

For Guruji walked and chanted too.

He walked to free our world from the destructive path we are walking on.

He said 'persevere' 'til the victory is won,

Through and through.

He made many friends on his journey,

The simple, the great and the small.

He walked amongst us for one hundred years.

He was gentle with the poor and kind-hearted.

His presence helped them overcome their fears.

Nor was he afraid to speak out

To the arrogant and the proud.

He would confront with his own body

Those whose actions would hurt all,

World 'round.

He said NO to the suffering. He said NO to war.

He said NO to bombs that kill and destroy.

He called all to a path where the precept is one.

A precept which says NO more killing.

NO more guns, no more weapons of destruction anymore.

He walked for a century.

Even The Crazy Man Wept

He walked 'til he could walk no more.

He walked, prayed and chanted until

He reached the other shore.

Now it's his sons and his daughters

Who carry on the walk.

It's through his daughters and sons

He continues to talk.

He challenges all our normal conceptions.

He says the change must come from within.

He calls for sacrifice, hard work

And loving hearts.

He asks much of his chosen few.

Yet they still walk in step,

And to the beat of a drum.

While not always understood,

It's always

A walk of love.

For they desire people to be free.

Free of all the suffering that we cause

To one another,

That we cause

To Thee.

They've allowed me to follow in their footsteps.

They've allowed me to walk as a friend.

They've shared how

And why they live the way they do,

On the walk that never ends.

I'm very attracted to their walk,

Though I don't know how to beat a drum.

I see all, the people they touch,

Even when the response is negative

Or none.

I've ate at their table.

I've prayed with them in the early morning sun.

I've listened to their struggles; I've listened to their fears.

I am peaceful in their presence.

I feel You are near.

Even The Crazy Man Wept

They've been willing to leave their own countries,

Be it by land,

Home or change of heart.

They are only human,

But the spark of the divine

Is clearly in their hearts.

It's too early for answers.

It's too early to say, 'now is the time', and, 'this is the place'.

It's a walk I'll continue on,

For I only desire to touch

And see your face.

It's clear they do not walk alone now.

It's clear they walk as one.

Whenever people walk and work

Together as they do,

The Kingdom has come.

Father God, Mother God, am I on the right path home now?

I will continue to ask.

But I hear my heart telling me,

It is here you could be

Free at last'.

It's been a privilege to walk in their footsteps,

A privilege to call them friends.

Privilege to meet such people,

On this walk

That never ends.

For now, be at peace in this temple,

In this peaceful home.

Give thanks to those you walk with,

For they are on the right path

Home.

Epilogue

An Eternity in Pure Love
by Edwin Pugh

'Do you know a Barang (*foreign*) man called Bob? He has lived and worked in
Cambodia to help the Khmer people all his life'.

The 'tuk tuk' driver produced one of those wide welcoming Khmer smiles
and replied in stuttering English, 'Oh, Mr Bob'. 'Yes, I know Mr Bob'.

'Where can I find him?' 'He always walking, always walking. But when in
Battambang he live at Wat (*Buddhist temple*) with monks'.

Here I was in November 2014 in the centre of Battambang City and the first
Cambodian I asked knew of my friend Bob. His reply beautifully summed up
Bob's life and love of the Khmer people. Bob, a Jesuit, had committed his
life to 'walk' with the poor people of Cambodia immediately after the dark,
dark, genocidal days of Cambodia's, 'Killing Fields'. His spiritual journey as a
Jesuit led him to 'walk' with the monks. With them he had completed several
Dhammayietra (*literally pilgrimage of truth*) journeys across a war ravaged
Cambodia. His home a quarter of a century later was with the monks in their
temple complex.

I need to qualify what is meant by 'home'. Bob lived in a mausoleum within
the temple complex. His home included the mausoleum balcony and a small
room; a larger room housed the interred bodies of the mausoleum owners.
They were kindly sharing their space with Bob. Bob's balcony allowed
unobstructed panoramic views over the temple crematorium and its
welcoming smoke-blackened oven doors 20 metres away. The crematorium
chimney, providing an exodus for the soul of the departed, proved a
memorable landmark and talking point.

'Bob, I have been involved with Cambodia since our days helping the
refugees back in the late 1980's. It's hard work. There is so much corruption.
Is it worth the effort?'

Bob doesn't like words. He finds them a distraction. He once told me,
'God's language is silence. Words are a poor substitute'. Words, he has

learnt, can cause all sorts of misunderstandings. Drawing on his long 'walk' with the Cambodian people he reflected then said bluntly, 'What you do is a drop in the ocean'. As my spirit plummeted he continued, 'but there would not be an ocean without the drops'. At this my spirit pulled out of its dive and I knew for certain that whatever the cost it was worthwhile.

Sipping a glass of water sitting on his balcony, watched over and overheard by the crematorium oven and its open door, Bob commented, 'I have had a long walk. I ain't getting any younger and the time will soon come when my walk will end'. He looked out from the balcony over the crematorium. 'At least they won't have to carry me very far', he wryly remarked. His future death was a reality he accepted with grace and peace.

'What do you think happens after you die, Bob?' 'We came from nothingness and will return to nothingness', was his response. I thought, given his Jesuit background he would be mentioning Heaven and God and Angels and the company of other saved souls.

'What will this nothingness be like? Will it be literally nothing? Will we know nothing?'

I saw Bob think a while and smile lovingly as he replied 'It will be an eternity of pure love'. And that was when I knew what Heaven was really about and who God was. Words were inadequate to describe it. But God is pure love and Heaven is living in an eternity of pure love. We need know no more to be comforted.

Our time together came to a rapid end. It was late evening and Bob had to walk to the Buddhist University nearby. The educational day had ended but Bob had a job cleaning classrooms and toilets to earn a living.

It was an emotional farewell, for me at least. It had been around ten years since we had last chatted and laughed together. Who knew how long it might be until we met again. At the bottom of the balcony steps we hugged, a brotherly hug. Emotionally choked I tried to say, 'Au revoir'. I think he heard. But then Bob gave another hug and said, 'No words'. In the silence that followed I experienced the reality of brotherly love and a knowledge that whether I see Bob again or not our souls will enjoy an eternity in pure love.

Links

This book with its message is being distributed at the lowest possible price and as often as possible, digital versions, will be available free of charge.

If the reader wishes to make a donation towards 'the poor' of Cambodia, this can be done through the charity **Transform Healthcare Cambodia**.

Simply log onto the website and various options for payment are given.

All monies donated will go directly to the work to improve the health of the poor in Cambodia.

www.transformhealthcarecambodia.org.uk

End Piece

On Christmas morning 1984, a young Jesuit, Bob Maat, began another day's work in Nong Samet, a camp. When he arrived he was faced with the sight of some 60,000 terrified people huddled in the ditch as the sound of shells thundered across the skies. The Vietnamese had launched a major attack.

Maat watched a woman help her sick husband with one arm and carry their two year old daughter with the other, their bag of essentials slung over her shoulder. The husband told his wife to leave him at the side of the road and carry on without him. The shells were landing closer. Crying, she refused to abandon him. People searched frantically among the crowds for their children and loved ones lost in the panic.

At the ditch the Thai soldiers were everywhere. The shells were getting closer and closer. Large clouds of smoke drifted over the refugees' heads. The camp was now burning and large flames leapt into the sky. A number of handicapped were seated together in the ditch; some in their wheelchairs, some with crutches. The trauma made some pregnant women go into labour. Matt who had been trained as a physician's assistant, helped deliver a baby boy among the crowds in the ditch. The shells were so close now that he could feel the percussion against his face as they landed. There were over twenty births in that ditch that morning. And more than 10,000 shells fell on the camp.

An extract from 'The Lost Executioner, A Story of the Khmer Rouge' by Nic Dunlop

ISBN 13 9780747566700 Hardback

ISBN 13 9780747580584 Paperback

A Movements Muffin

'Movements Muffins' are a new type of digital *(and sometimes a slim paperback)* book. They are aimed at readers on the move and are designed to tempt you to want to know more about a range of positive subjects. 'Muffins' are mainly, but not always, non-fiction. So why not settle down with a coffee and a 'Muffin', and widen your horizons.

To discover more of our publications, check out our website, **www.movements.me.uk** periodically.

Even The Crazy Man Wept

Reflections following the War in Cambodia

By Dr Edwin Pugh

Kindle ISBN - 978 1 898650 51 5

ePub ISBN - 978 1 898650 52 2

Paperback ISBN - 978 1 898650 53 9

Part of the Movements Muffins 'Inspired Lives' Series